GEORGE HUDSON AND WHITBY

GEORGE HUDSON
AND
WHITBY

——

CORDELIA STAMP

The evil that men do lives on
The good is oft interred with their bones

CAEDMON OF WHITBY

First published 2005 by
Caedmon of Whitby
128 Upgang Lane, Whitby YO21 3JJ

ISBN 0905355 63 6

Printed by Smith Settle Printing and Bookbinding Ltd.
Ilkley Road, Otley, LS21 3JP

GEORGE HUDSON

George Hudson became motherless at the age of six and within a couple more years his father also died, leaving the orphan to the care of his elder brothers, John and William, who had then to run the farm at Howsham, and presumably his elder sisters did their best to mother their young siblings.

But there is no real substitute for parental love and care as well as discipline. By the time the boy entered his teens he was pretty much left to his own devices. If his elders tried to discipline him it would seem they were unsuccessful, for at fifteen he was – or rather the girl was – in Trouble (as the phrase has it.) The Poor Book of the time records a payment 'received from George Hudson for Bastardy, 12s 6d'. In the same year both his elder sisters died.

After this episode, of which we know no more of the child or its mother, the erring boy was sent away to York to make his own way in the world. Like Dick Whittington he may well have heard the same ditty promising a rosy future; indeed, he too also became a lord mayor.

In the noble city of York dwelt one Matthew Bottrill, brother of George's grandmother and therefore his mother's uncle. He was born in Bugthorpe in the same area as Howsham. He was a man of property and lived in a fine Georgian house in Monkgate and in the accepted terminology of the time is simply described as a 'gentleman', a soubriquet perhaps for 'wealthy'.

It would be very likely that, having no children of his own, Great Uncle Matthew would take kindly to young George, who perhaps reminded him of his own sister, Ann. It is quite possible that his inborn paternal feelings would be transferred to the boy. Likewise, it is possible that George would find in his great uncle the kindly parental discipline which had been so lacking in his own youth.

Be that as it may, by one way or another, George started work in Bell and Nicholson's drapers shop. Years spent behind a shop counter are one of the best training grounds in life. University may be all very well, but one is surrounded by contemporaries there and the sudden release from strict school discipline is not always beneficial. In a shop not only does one meet all sorts and conditions of people, but one learns, often very quickly, just how best to deal with them without being over subservient or too assertive. O yes, the customer must always be right.

These lessons would be of use to young George and he settled happily into the draper's life, working with the owner's widow, Rachel Bell, her brother Richard and sister Elizabeth Nicholson. It is not recorded, in those pre-census days, where George lived at this time. Possibly with Great Uncle Matthew, or maybe in lodgings. The days of Dickens's accounts of sleeping under the shop counter were long past, and perhaps he lived above the shop. Certain it is that he eventually did live there, for shortly after his 21st birthday he and Richard's sister Elizabeth were married.

Rachel Bell retired and gave the business to her brother and George as partners and it became Nicholson and Hudson. Richard and George between them made a settlement payment of six thousand pounds. Part of this amount would include the existing stock in the shop, but there would also be a cash settlement. It is most unlikely that George's part of this would be from the farm at Howsham, for John, the eldest son, already had that which today is euphemistically called a 'drink problem' and prosperity and inebriation do not go together. It seems much more likely that the payment would come from Matthew Bottrill.

In his excellent biography, Robert Beaumont has pointed out that the Hudson's first three babies, born in the College Street shop, did not survive or thrive as did those born later, after their parents had moved to a more salubrious home in Monkgate. This came about after Matthew Bottrill had died and left his house to them.

In what proved to be Matthew's last illness George and Elizabeth were his constant attendants, and we must ascribe this to their affection and concern for their elderly relative, rather than that which some snide writers have inferred of their casting a monetary eye on the wealthy invalid's property. George had, after all, been a sort of son to the childless Matthew and it is hard to believe that he was directly involved in the old man's changing of his will.

But change it he did.

THE GEORGIAN MONKGATE HOUSE
Built in 1743, where Matthew Bottrill lived for many years before his death in 1827 and which he bequeathed to Hudson.
(Photograph by kind permission of Rita Bailey)

MATTHEW BOTTRILL'S WILL

Many and varied are the accounts of George Hudson's legacy which are given by the growing army of biographers. Most estimate the amount of money left to him as thirty thousand pounds, but there are no actual written figures to support this assertion. All gleefully repeat each other in that figure as well as the Whitby property myth.

Bottrill's will itself is clear enough. Whilst it mentions 'Real estate situated at Osbaldwick and Huntington', nothing is said about Whitby. He leaves his gold watch to 'Richard, son of George Hudson' and one can well imagine Uncle Matthew attracting the infant's attention by swinging his watch to and fro and enjoying its little baby chuckles.

As well as an annuity, he left his housekeeper 'The clothes and wearing apparel of my late wife and the small silver cup which she commonly used.' This last was the first clue we had to indicate that Bottrill had been married and there is no record of any issue. It turns out that he had married Ann Wilberfoss of Stockton on Forest in 1783. She died in 1823 and was buried in Holy Trinity, Goodramgate.

The final page in this will is one which puzzles me greatly. It is dated five months after Bottrill's death and reads:–

> 'The whole of the goods, chattels and credits of the said deceased do not amount in value to the sum of ten thousand pounds.'

It is signed by Robert Sutton, Surrogate.

So who invented the figure of thirty thousand pounds.?

A man who had such well formed and clear handwriting and capability of expressing himself lucidly must to my mind, have had some primary education other than that shown by kindly aunts and siblings. I found it hard to believe that those who claim the title of biographer had firmly stated that there was no school at Howsham. Particularly as the family who lived in the Hall were Cholmleys, who also owned the fine Abbey House,

THE OLD SCHOOL AT HOWSHAM

Having been sympathetically converted inside, it is now a private dwelling house. It is probable that the next door cottage was originally the school teacher's home.

built in Tudor times after the dissolution of the monasteries with use made of the abbey stones, standing on Whitby's cliff top surrounded by the Abbey Plain.

Lady Cholmley founded a school for Whitby children in the 19th century in Church Street, fronting the River Esk, which today has become the home of the Friendship Rowing Club. I reasoned to myself that if a member of that family had an educational concern, maybe it was likely that the same might have happened in Howsham before the days of the Education Act, where the lord of the manor was a Cholmley.

So I hied me to Howsham and almost the very first building I met with was the small village school. An inset stone told me that it had been REbuilt by Colonel Cholmley in 1852. Not built, mark you, but RE built. Which presupposes that there must have been a school of sorts standing there before this time.

I was delighted also to find that the Cholmley's beautiful Jacobean mansion was not only still standing but also proving its usefulness, to the joy

HOWSHAM HALL
The Jacobean residence of Sir John Wentworth, whose daughter married Hugh Cholmley whereby the hall and its estate passed to the Cholmleys. The estate was bought by the Strickland family later and the hall is now a prep school.

of Lady Cholmley's ghost, by housing a thriving present day prep school.

Scrayingham Church was not far down the road and there I found the distinctive grey marble tomb where rest the remains of George, his wife Elizabeth and three of their infant children. Nearby lie his father, John, his mother Elizabeth, his sisters Mary and Elizabeth and his brother William.

My second graveyard safari took me to Bugthorpe, a few miles along from Scrayingham. This was where Matthew Bottrill had been born and was buried and I had great hopes of finding his wife's name on his tombstone. But No. The only evidence of his resting place was a great flat, heavy stone laid in the church's grassy burial ground with the sole inscription:

M.BOTTRILL ESQ
VAULT
1827

Standing beside this there was an upright tombstone recording the death of his father Thomas Bottrill 1721–1807. I would dearly have liked to find a stone record of Matthew's mother, Ann (Hannah), but I simply have to rely on old parish records which tell us that her maiden name was Hudson.

When I saw this blank stone my personal estimation of George Hudson plummeted some-what, for he was the sole executor of his benevolent great uncle and yet he had refrained from having any family details placed on the tombstone, – or should I say vaultstone, for there is a subtle, and costlier, difference in the terms. I could not but feel that George may well have thought; 'Well, he's gone now and I've got the money.' Surely, any decent person would have placed something more than the isolated record of a date and surname only. To myself, the omission was highly indicative of an indifference and lack of consideration for others which must have lain in George's nature along with his other characteristics.

What is certain is that after receiving his legacy, George Hudson gave up the drapers shop and moved to the Monkgate house. He became a councillor and then an alderman in the ancient city of York. He was elected lord mayor twice, in 1838 and 1839 and then for a third time in 1846, when he was deep in his railway promotions.

It is not the purpose of this little book to enter into the wheeling and dealing of Hudson's railway enterprises, but rather to discover where, when and how he became involved with Whitby and to that end it has been decided to speak mainly about his Whitby connection.

Information about Hudson's Whitby activities is non-existent before he joined the Whitby Building Company in the 1830s. It is repeatedly said that he had been left 'Whitby Property' by his great uncle. I have been unable to find any information, written or spoken, about this ephemeral property, if any.

The biographers repeatedly make the assertion that 'he spent holidays in Whitby' and, in the all too common manner found in so many writers, A repeats what B said who copies C who said that D mentioned … and so on. But none of these assertions are supported by any evidence of the original fact. To this noble army may I commend the more frequent use, when they are pursuing the great unknown, of the following words: perhaps, maybe, probably, no possible doubt whatever.

For myself, I find it is probably untrue that George Hudson and/or his family did spend holidays in Whitby. Just for a start, there were no passenger trains then. Transport would have been by rattling coach on dubious roads at one or two horse power. Fifty miles was almost a day's journey. Macadam roads only started in 1815 and probably did not reach Whitby for another thirty years at least. (By which time the railways were providing smoother travel.)

Apart from that, the Hudsons were running their small business in the York drapers shop, so who would run it in their absence?

If we are to believe his biographers it would seem that Hudson had many holidays both before and after the days of simplified travel. Arnold & McCartney note that:

'He went to Paris, where he had spent family holidays in the past.' (p220)

When? I wonder.

opposite page: **THE LORD MAYOR OF YORK**
Seen in the Mansion House with his family in 1839.
L to R: Elizabeth, William, John, George, Ann and George Hudson.
St Helen's Church is just visible through the window and the oil
painting is of King William III.

Oh what a tangled web we weave
When first we practise to deceive

It is not for me to untangle this web, being, as I am, so unfamiliar with the practice of buying and selling shares. All I can recall is Mr Stapleton telling us about the South Sea Bubble in history lessons at school, and my own father's misfortune with one Hatry.

Hudson's misdoings have been compared to those of Clarence Hatry. I was quite relieved to find that Hudson's name was not included in Brewers *Dictionary of Rogues*. However, Hatry's was, and deservedly so, for he was an undoubted rogue and got a sentence of fourteen years hard labour at the Old Bailey. There was no reparation for the thousands of share holders, my father among them. I was sorry to see that Hatry served only nine years of his sentence and then he was out, in his old haunts and up to his old tricks.

Hudson did not defraud anyone or invent fraudulent companies. His rail companies were real enough, it was simply that the returns did not come up to the expected profits. At one time he was so bewildered by the small returns that he paid the shareholders a dividend by using money from the capital account rather than let them down. His middle name should have been Micawber.

I am in sympathy with many of Hudson's misdemeanours. When, for example, he bought enormous quantities of iron rails, in his own name, at the rate of nine pounds per ton and later re-sold them to the railway company at twelve pounds per ton, he was doing no more than most shopkeepers who would, quite legitimately, add their recognised percentage, usually 25%, to stock which they had bought at trade price, in order to arrive at the retail price. So if one is to condemn a man for doing this, then Napoleon's 'nation of shopkeepers' is in for a hard time.

One move which Hudson made, which he must have thought most astute, was in 1845 when he bought the 12,000 acre Londesborough Estate.

Some time later the new railway needed to cross part of the estate. As its new owner he claimed and pocketed the eventual compensation fees.

It was the accepted practice for land owners to give their permission for the new railway to cross their land. As a general rule it was Hudson himself who visited them and presented them with a weighty wallet of notes. These he had drawn from his own bank, which he owned, and he charged the railway company accordingly. He also happened to be the director of that company.

None of his actions were deliberately criminal. Being morally wrong is not an indictable offence, but unfortunately for him, owing large sums of money without repayment was, and the law put insolvent debtors into jail.

Put in the very simplest terms possible, my own view is as follows: Money was borrowed in order to pay for:

Surveying the land for routes
Building the actual tracks
Building bridges, stations, platforms &c
Erecting very numerous station houses and
Level crossing houses &c
Rolling stock
Staffing
Wages
Labour

The last item on the long list of outgoings is that which covers Hudson's greatest achievement. He supplied employment for yet another long list of workers. Labourers, navvies, masons, craftsmen, engineers, train staff: drivers, stokers, guards, porters. Their wages were paid and dinners supplied to their families, whilst the shareholders were obliged to wait for the promised payout they blindly hoped for.

The principal suppliers of these funds were moneylenders in the guise of 1) Banks and

2) Shareholders. The railway company held out vast promises of immense profits once the system had got under way. But it did not take long to realise that the out-going expenses greatly exceeded the in-coming returns. Those who had let greed govern their actions were quick to turn round and look for the culprit whom they thought had misled them.

At the start of the Railway Mania, George Hudson could do no wrong. As the truth began to dawn over the ensuing years that there was no endless fountain of immortal drink after all, he then became the target of all the investors' spleen and he was hated where before he had been adulated.

GEORGE HUDSON, LORD MAYOR OF YORK
Painted by Sir Francis Grant, the portrait hangs in York's Mansion House and is reproduced by their kind permission.

THE WHITBY CONNECTION

As early as 1827 there were suggestions being made about the development needed in Whitby 'to accommodate strangers who may wish to reside in our good town during the bathing season.' Meetings were held and various committees were formed, but for quite a while the only action was Talk, more Talk and yet more meetings. A Joint Stock Company was formed, but very little progress was made. It was not until 1843 that George Hudson, – although in the midst of railway speculation and aldermanic duties – came to Whitby and set up the Whitby Building Company.

Although Action This Day was one of Churchill's favourite orders, Hudson could not do the same and matters had to simmer whilst he became MP for Sunderland and saw to the construction of their docks, not the smallest part of which was the promoting of shares to support the venture.

Finally, in 1848, the Whitby Building Company bought the entire West Cliff Estate and its development seemed nearer to becoming a reality. Hudson had to take out huge loans for this enterprise, but he knew, – and hoped – that eventually the erection of houses and hotels would justify the outgoing.

The very first proposals for the project, in 1827, had suggested that:

> The most eligible situation for lodging houses would be some part of the Cliff Fields, near the flagstaff. Wherever they are erected, let them not be built of brick but of polished or dressed stone, which is incomparably more beautiful, that, like the Gas House and the Bath building, they may be an ornament to Whitby.

It is hard to imagine the freedom from bureaucratic interference and restraint which would-be developers enjoyed a hundred and fifty years ago. When Hudson came to Whitby he had a vision of what might be done to develop the place as a resort and he was able to set about implementing his plan without restriction.

The first item on his agenda was to build a large hotel to accommodate the anticipated influx of holiday visitors. So the Royal Hotel was built alongside an equally imposing terrace and East Crescent. One of the first families to occupy no 6 East Terrace was that of Charles Hudson, his younger brother who was to manage the new hotel.

The official architect to the whole project was John Dobson renowned for his design of Newcastle's Central Station. After the Royal Hotel came the proposed 'Boarding Houses' on the West Cliff Estate. Topped and tailed by Langdale Terrace at one end and Belle Vue Terrace at the other, there are four adjoining streets John Street, Normanby Terrace, Abbey Terrace and – unlike its York counterpart which lost its original title – the last one still retains its first intended name of Hudson Street, in honour of its innovator.

The first committee's intention of using stone for the buildings proved to be a difficult undertaking, due to a combination of quarry availability, carriage, haulage problems, but largely that of expense. Hudson decided not only to use bricks, but to manufacture them as well, using the plentiful local clay. Objectors to this scheme were not wanting. Nevertheless, up went the houses.

Intending purchasers of the new properties, including those who bought building plots only, were plentiful, but they were strictly bound by legal requirements regarding the limitations of the proposed structure.

> Any building erected thereon shall not be used for the sale of ale beers wine spirits or any other intoxicating liquor nor for the sale of flesh fish vegetables or any other corruptible provisions or articles nor for a butchers slaughter house livery stable or public auction room nor any trade or business in which a steam engine is required ... whereby any noise smell or other inconvenience may be heard smelt or perceived.

All of which makes one wonder why lawyers did not use commas.

As his ultimate accolade Hudson had planned the erection of a magnificent crescent which would equal, if not outshine that of Bath. Alas! Halfway through this endeavour his best laid schemes went sadly agley. He owed the money lenders vast amounts and they, – to their shame – had continued advancing him more money and so sooner or later the bubble was bound to burst. The West Cliff Estate had been used as security for Hudson's loans from the railway companies and so it ultimately fell into their hands. Thus it is that today, a hundred and fifty years later, Royal Crescent remains only half completed.

ROYAL HOTEL, WEST CLIFF.

THE ROYAL HOTEL, WHITBY
As it was in 1895 before the present day loggia was added. It is likely that the railings were removed for the war time scrap iron drive. (Whitby Archives)

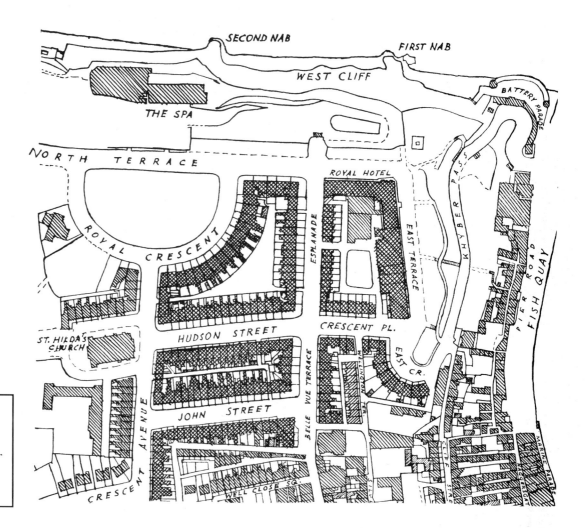

SECOND NAB
FIRST NAB

WEST CLIFF

BATTERY PARADE

THE SPA

NORTH TERRACE

ROYAL HOTEL

ROYAL CRESCENT

ESPLANADE

EAST TERRACE

KHYBER PASS

PIER ROAD

FISH QUAY

ST. HILDA'S CHURCH

HUDSON STREET

CRESCENT PL.

EAST CR.

WELLINGTON TERR.

BELLE VUE TERRACE

JOHN STREET

CRESCENT AVENUE

WELL CLOSE SQ.

CLIFF STREET

MARINE PARADE

THE WEST CLIFF
ESTATE
The chart which appears in the
1958 SURVEY OF WHITBY
(By kind permission of the
Marquis of Normanby).

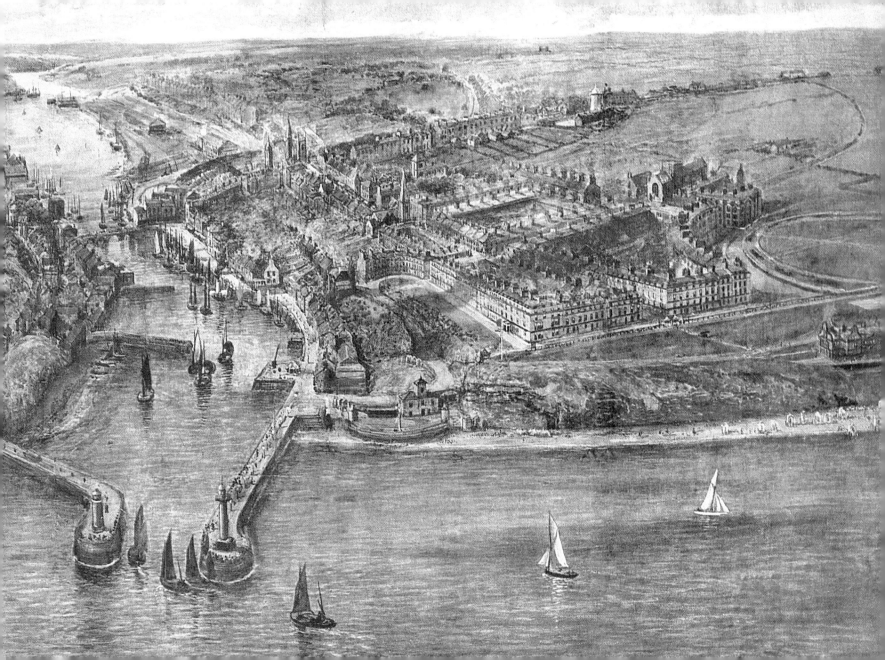

Despite all the mud thrown in his direction after the collapse of the railway bubble, Hudson's greatest faults were sins of omission.

He 'forgot' to enter details of acquisitions in his accounts. He omitted having the services of qualified accountants to audit his books. O yes, he did say that his books were open to inspection by any shareholder, but did they have experienced knowledge of accounting? He failed to record the amounts paid hither and yon to greedy landowners. He didn't mention This and he said nothing about That.

I like the epigram quoted by Lambert:

How was Midas ruined?
By keeping everything but his accounts.

If any man needed the services of an accountant it was George Hudson. He, however was an archetypical loner. At one time in replying to a question about his allocation of railway shares to investors in the Whitby Building Company he said:

I had no motive but to do what was right.

As a member of parliament Hudson was exempt from arrest for debt, but in 1859 he lost his Sunderland seat and so was obliged to flee to France to avoid arrest. His ever faithful wife remained in London, living on her marriage settlement which could not be taken by debt collectors.

Their three sons, George, John and William had all completed their education at Harrow and Christchurch shortly before their father's collapse. George became a barrister and lived at Ascot, John joined the army and was killed at the age of 25 in the Indian Mutiny, while William became a doctor and lived with his mother in London. He too was tragically killed in a train accident.

Looking towards the future for his three sons Hudson had bought estates in Yorkshire for their eventual use. These were: Baldersby, near Ripon; Octon Grange, near Bridlington; Newby Park, near Thirsk, into which he moved himself, and he also bought Londesborough Park, near Market Weighton, from the Duke of Devonshire; its hall had been demolished some forty years before and Hudson intended building a grand mansion in its place. To manage the estate he installed his younger brother, Charles, who lived in the small shooting lodge with his growing family. From there, Charles came to Whitby to manage his brother's newly built Royal Hotel.

Unfortunately, in 1864 he died suddenly and George risked returning to England for a flying visit to see to the funeral and arrange matters at his Royal Hotel. It was Christmas time in 1864 and Hudson managed to return to France without being arrested.

In the following summer there was to be an election and Hudson decided to stand as the Tory candidate for Whitby. The seat was held by the Liberal party's man, H.S. Thompson. Unpopular was hardly the word to describe his seven year reign. Whitby people rightly felt that he constantly gave precedence to Scarborough. A popular jingle of that time was:

> Bundle Thompson off to Scarbro' by train,
> That's where all his cheap trips went,
> And where their brass was spent,
> And he'll do the same again.
> Whitby lads, he'll cut you all again.

Traditionally Whitby has always been and still is a conservative town and Hudson's return in 1865 as the prospective Tory candidate was rapturously received. Crowds gathered to welcome him outside the Angel Hotel and he made a short speech anticipating his address to the people that evening.

This took place at the newly opened St Hilda's Hall behind the Angel Hotel. We are fortunate in having the whole of that address rather than abbreviated press versions. It is such a striking defence of his own actions in the face of adversity that it is right that it should be printed here in its entirety.

HUDSON'S OWN DEFENCE

Gentlemen, my character has been assailed. That attack was founded on a report of the Eastern Counties Railway in 1849. My object in going into that undertaking was to consolidate the railway system. A man cannot always succeed in his object and I did not succeed in that. A committee was appointed and the report they drew up was founded on utter falsehood. They stated that I had altered the accounts, but I, at this meeting, utterly deny it, and in giving it the lie here, I not only speak to the meeting, but to the world at large. (cheers).

These accounts were never altered by me and I had nothing whatever to do with them. Now, I am in a position to bring up as evidence the late secretary of the company who says that the accounts were not falsified by me.

Founded on that report a petition was presented to the House of Commons, of which I was then a member, asking for a committee of inquiry. I answered that petition by stating my readiness to vote for the inquiry. I denied the accusation against me in my place in the House, and in so doing I received the universal cheers of that august assembly. (Applause)

Gentlemen, I was prepared to defend my character and my honour as one of the members of parliament, if it had been allowed me; but the members of the House so warmly cheered me on all sides that it was clear they did not believe one word that was said against me. (Cheers)

At that time, gentlemen, I had not the evidence in my favour that I now possess; but as time has rolled on I have secured the authority of a person, no less than the secretary of the company, to state that I never altered the accounts, and that the charge against me was a complete and entire fabrication.

It showed the animus that actuated men's minds opposed to me at that day, for it was a time when men's consciences and judgments were warped, and when malice and all sorts of unkindness predominated against me.

Before they published that report they ought to have asked me:– 'Did you alter these figures, Sir, are these altered figures, Sir?' If they had done so they would have received the answer of denial that was necessary. (Cheers) But they did not. (Cheers) The figures were not mine, I never made them in my life, and two excellent friends of mine who had seen them have told me, 'I know your figures and I know your writing; but these figures and this writing are not yours.' (Loud cheers)

Then there was the **Midland report**. No blame attached to me with regard to the Midland line, but malice upon malice was heaped upon me relative to that concern.

I was the principal and chief manager of this railway, and in the report of the Committee of Investigation not a single word of reproach was uttered against me. Then why should an attempt be made to injure my character as regards the Midland railway after the enormous benefits which I conferred upon that company? When I entered upon the management of that concern it consisted of three rival companies – they were torn with distraction and with competition which was throwing the property away.

I took a course which was new in railway management then; but which is now perfectly well understood and generally adopted. I made them unite themselves together and become friends and not enemies. I have now the satisfaction of feeling that what I did was for the best, and that I was in the right, that the policy was characterised by wisdom and foresight; and if the railway world owes me no other debt of gratitude, at all events I can claim from it the merit of founding a system which has worked so admirably in the consolidation of these great advantages, and has conferred not only great benefits on the companies, but also on the public at large. The Midland shares were then down below 50, and by my policy they then rose up to 190. I will ask, was that no saving of property; did the widow and the orphan suffer in that case? No, gentlemen, the widow and orphan were made to rejoice by the course of conduct which I took on that occasion. (Applause)

There were gentlemen upon that committee, gentlemen of first rate integrity and intelligence, and Mr Arkwright was their chairman. They employed a public accountant, a man of ability, and he went through and over everything, fishing and ferreting about. He stated that such and such things ought to be charged to revenue which were put down as capital. Not having any malice or bad feeling against me, the committee repudiated the proposition of their accountant as being untenable, and through their chairman, Mr Arkwright, they declared that the accounts were fairly and honestly made out and perfectly correct. (Cheers)

Then there was the **York and North Midland report**. A report to which I entirely objected because the accounts were quite right. The company was properly managed and in a prosperous condition when I vacated the chair. You are all well aware that persons connected with trade experience from time to time periods of prosperity and periods of depression or loss, and therefore how was it possible for me to ensure constant sunshine in these large railway undertakings any more than it is possible to secure continued prosperity in trade and commerce?

Railways must depend upon the prosperity of the country. If the tradesmen, the manufacturer, the ironmaster or the artisan suffer, why the railways must suffer too. (Hear Hear)

With regard to the **Newcastle and Berwick** line, I could weep on thinking how deeply painful the course of that company has been. One of the charges against me respecting it was that I was extending its unprofitableness and mismanaging it merely for electioneering purposes at Sunderland. I was accused of having fixed a tariff of rates giving to that place a priority over other ports, and I was charged with having done so to promote my political position as its representative. But what was the fact?

The new management altered these rates, but in less than twelve months they were obliged to revert back to my rates of charges, finding that otherwise they would suffer an enormous loss of traffic and revenue. (Cheers)

There was another point. I had taken a large amount of dock shares for the company, and I had the foresight to see that they would be extremely valuable in an indirect manner to the company. I wished the company to be a master of that dock, but the shares were repudiated by the Committee of Inquiry and forced upon me, by which I lost a sum of at least £80,000. And what did the company gain? The effect of their policy was to admit a serious competition, which abstracted from the North Eastern Railway a revenue of at least £30,000 a year. The result has shown that I was in the right and that they were in the wrong with respect to the Sunderland docks, and they used me cruelly by forcing me to take £80,000 of dock shares.

Then there is the **Newcastle and Carlisle Railway**. I took that railway in hand on an arrangement to pay its shareholders six percent and worked it as part of the North Eastern system. The committee, men without any commercial experience and knowledge, said that they would have nothing to do with it, that I might take it and get rid of it, and I had to do so at a loss of £12,000 to myself. Since then, however, the line has been taken by them, and eight per cent is now being paid for it.

I also took **Maryport and Carlisle Railway** at four per cent for a term, with an increase of six per cent ultimately. The committee advised the shareholders of the Newcastle and Berwick Company to reject the beneficial arrangement and they did so. From that contract I was relieved without loss. The Carlisle and Maryport line has had such an element of prosperity about it ever since that it has paid from eight to eleven per cent. (Hear Hear) This proves the wisdom of my policy.

Instead, then, of oppressing me, – a single individual – with an iron hand, and extracting from me the last drop of blood, they ought to have adopted an entirely different course towards me. They have thrown away, by their weakness, malice and folly, hundreds and thousands of pounds, in pressing down one who has done them no harm, and in seeking to ruin and send me into poverty. (Cheers)

Then there is again the Stockton and Darlington line, which I had arranged for at five per cent and it is now paying nine or ten. These are facts, I think, which will tell your minds that the course I pursued has been the right one. Time has shown that my policy was wise, and that I have not been actuated by the motives which these men attributed to me. (Hear Hear)

It has often been said, how many families have been ruined by me; but I will ask how many families have been saved by my policy? How many think you? I have made upwards of twenty millions of property safe and secure, and thousands of families receive their dividends with as much certainty as if they had their money invested in the funds. No speculation of this class can be looked upon as blessed with complete success; and although loss may have been sustained by a few individuals, yet I look back with wonder and astonishment to find that all my schemes and plans have borne such rich fruit, and that the railways with which I was connected have stood better than almost any other railway property in the kingdom. (Applause)

It is always disagreeable to speak of oneself, but I am obliged to do so in this assembly of my friends to vindicate my character. I have longed from the bottom of my heart, for years, to have the opportunity of telling the electors of Whitby of my wrongs, and in doing so, to defend myself, and I am proud to have the chance of saying these few words to you. (Cheers)

It has been seriously said that I purposely depreciated the value of the property of which I had the management. Why, gentlemen, it is absurd to talk of depreciation. I am old enough to recollect well when the Great Western shares were at £180 premium, which were worth £60 paid, made them £240. What is the price of them now? They are at 70 and I have seen them down at 47. They might charge the chairman of the Great Western with depreciation of the value of property with greater force than they do me.

There is another line, the **London and North Western**. I remember when the shares were at 380 and afterwards they went down to about 100. Now they are about 120. Do they charge the

London and North Western chairman with the same charges they bring against me? No. The fact is, gentlemen, I have been made the scapegoat for the sins of the people, but I have borne all of the obloquy showered upon me with much courage and strength of mind, and my innocence has been a great support to me in the persecutions I have undergone. I can tell all my enemies and detractors that I can bear their malice, however long continued, with the same sang-froid as I have endured attacks from much abler men. (Cheers)

GEORGE HUDSON

Painted by G R Ward very largely taken from the Grant portrait, this picture is now in the National Portrait Gallery, by whose kind permission it is shown.

WHITBY WEST CLIFF FROM THE AIR
This photograph clearly shows the extent of Hudson's enterprise.

There is no hatred in the world so great as that of ignorance for knowledge, Gallileo said, but coming a close second to that is the hatred of success by those who have failed.

This was undoubtedly the case with H. S. Thompson who feared and hated Hudson with the greatest venom. Despite his tissue-thin denials he it was who engineered Hudson's downfall at this election in 1865. A trumped up creditor was discovered to whom Hudson owed some money and only two days before polling took place, in the early morning, Hudson was awakened, arrested, and taken on the first train to York, where he was imprisoned in York Castle.

He languished there for three long months. His outstanding debt was finally paid by a good friend, George Elliot of Houghton Hall, a colliery owner. He was later knighted and long afterwards he became the ultimate purchaser of the Whitby Estate. Not only that, he it was who organised a subscription to buy an annuity to support Hudson in his exile.

It is some comfort to know that H. S. Thompson did not retain his Whitby seat, for the Whitby conservative party quickly substituted Charles Bagnall and he was returned.

Hudson tried a second flying visit to England in 1868 to try and sort out matters with his creditors, the North Eastern Railway Company, only to be arrested once more and put in the London debtors prison. He was enabled to be released under an ancient ruling, dating from the Magna Carta, which allowed him time to take legal advice. Wasting no further time, George returned to France.

At the beginning of 1870, – a year remembered for the death of Dickens as well as a new Education Act, another Act came into force, namely the Abolition of Imprisonment for Debt Act. This meant that Hudson could now safely return to his homeland, so he had at least two more years to live in peace. There was now no need to seek to re-enter parliament in order to avoid arrest.

He settled with his wife in her London home and, despite his gout and angina, enjoyed his final years and eventually became free of debt.

After a visit to his old Northern haunts in the autumn of 1871 he had a further angina attack and on the 14th of December, exactly eight years to the day after his brother Charles died, he died in the arms of his son William, the doctor. His life ended but his fame remained. He was to be buried in the family vault at Scrayingham and his coffin was transported to York station, where the funeral procession started.

The hearse was drawn by four horses, without any nodding plumes as Hudson and his wife had directed, and made its slow way to Scrayingham, through the city where the tradesmen showed their respect by keeping the shutters up and the blinds down. It was St Thomas's day and the Gazette commented:

> Throughout the day the sun shone with a brilliancy rarely witnessed on the shortest day of the year. Thus closed in calmness and in peace the last scene of one who ... had filled so prominent a position among his fellow men.

... ...

At one time there was talk of erecting a monument to Hudson. What eventually arrived was a statue of his arch enemy, George Leeman. Hudson's enduring memorial in Whitby is the half completed Royal Crescent, the start of his dream and its final collapse.

ROYAL CRESCENT
Another aerial photograph shows Hudson's lasting memorial, the half completed Royal Crescent. It is fitting that the row of houses immediately behind is called Hudson Street.

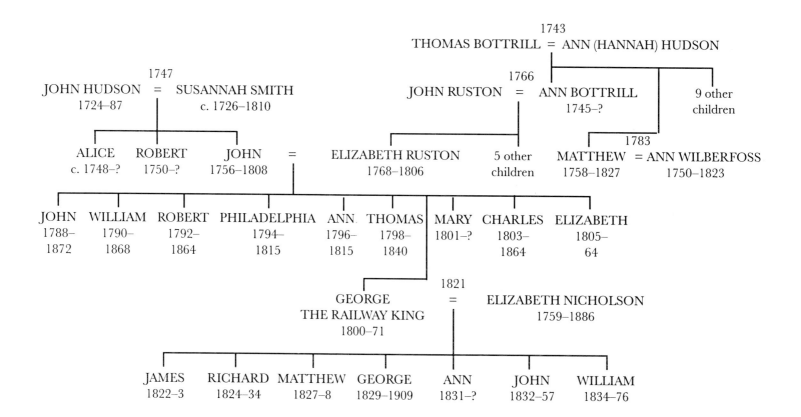

1743
THOMAS BOTTRILL = ANN (HANNAH) HUDSON

1747
JOHN HUDSON = SUSANNAH SMITH
1724–87   c. 1726–1810

1766
JOHN RUSTON = ANN BOTTRILL   9 other
                              1745–?   children

ALICE   ROBERT   JOHN   =   ELIZABETH RUSTON   5 other   MATTHEW = ANN WILBERFOSS
c. 1748–?   1750–?   1756–1808   1768–1806   children   1758–1827   1750–1823

1783

JOHN   WILLIAM   ROBERT   PHILADELPHIA   ANN   THOMAS   MARY   CHARLES   ELIZABETH
1788–   1790–   1792–   1794–   1796–   1798–   1801–?   1803–   1805–
1872   1868   1864   1815   1815   1840   1864   64

1821
GEORGE   =   ELIZABETH NICHOLSON
THE RAILWAY KING   1759–1886
1800–71

JAMES   RICHARD   MATTHEW   GEORGE   ANN   JOHN   WILLIAM
1822–3   1824–34   1827–8   1829–1909   1831–?   1832–57   1834–76

JOHN PRIDE

Nobody liked John Pride
Until he died.
Then everybody said
Poor John's dead.

And when he'd gone
They found that John
Had often done
Good for fun.

Which only shows
That nobody knows.

John Drinkwater

ACKNOWLEDGEMENTS

My thanks are due to Sylvia Hutchinson and Colin Waters of the Whitby Archives; Margaret Bottrill Holmes, the veritable wizard of family tree research; as well as that other wizard of Otley, Ken Smith printer non pareil, and his team; County archives at Northallerton and Beverley; the Borthwick Institute and also the librarians at Scarborough and Whitby, who understand the intricacies of computers as well as retaining their original devotion to the printed word.

Although I may perhaps be rather too critical of previous writers of the Hudson story, I am still grateful to them all for the enormous lot of work they have done.

Their names are:

R S Lambert	The Railway King	1934
A J Peacock	George Hudson	1988
Brian Bailey	George Hudson	1995
Robert Beaumont	The Railway King	2002
Arnold & McCartney	George Hudson	2004

Cover picture is by F M Sutcliffe, the renowned Whitby artist behind the camera lens. My thanks are due to Mike Shaw and the Sutcliffe Gallery for permission to reproduce it here.